Lancashire RECIPES Old & New

Collected and compiled by

Catherine Rothwell

Dedicated to My Dear Mother.

Contents

Published by Countryside Publications Limited, School Lane, Brinscall, Chorley, Lancashire.

Printed by Tamley-Reed Limited.

ISBN 0 86157 018 9

Introduction

This book harks back to the days of simple, old-fashioned cooking in fire ovens, for many of these family recipes are 60–90 years old and more. However, any of the dishes can be made in modern ovens and the best of both worlds can be yours, using labour-saving appliances to take the hard work out of chopping, blending, creaming. Generally speaking, results will be as delicious and nutritious as they were in great-grandmother's day because all are well-tried recipes that have stood the test of time.

Nineteenth century eel pie, to which the Victorians were very partial, was prepared in much the same way in the eighteenth century and probably even before. To own a river, three acres and a cow, was always an advantage and eels are now less easy to come by, but the true enthusiast will not be deterred. Often a substitute ingredient can be found. The brightest jewel in Aunt Kate's crown and gleaming from her "receeps" was Imagination. She wedded the lowly to the high, using, for instance, pigs' trotters to make more succulent the rather dry meat of pheasant. What is fundamental to *all* the recipes that follow is that they embody good, fresh, wholesome food prepared cleanly, briskly and with the minimum of standing and handling.

I firmly believe that food bought fresh, prepared lovingly and presented within a short time of purchase proves most popular and satisfies the body best, and in these respects both the old, established, recipes and the new ones are the same. If you are a devotee of the deep-freeze, convenience-food syndrome, this book is not meant for you unless, hopefully, it wins you over to more old-fashioned ways.

However many times you dish up a family favourite it never seems boring or repetitive, and the pleasure of seeing a well-timed, savoury meal vanish with sighs of satisfaction is its own reward. So, too, is the sight of a child taking food again following an illness, or resting easy after a sore throat on a foggy, winter's night; the recipes and remedies used to bring such things about are as successful now as half a century ago.

Yet it is the simple things that are soonest forgotten, or never experienced: the pleasure of a coal fire; the taste of toast made on a fork over glowing embers; the aroma of chestnuts roasting; of kippers cooked on a griddle; of home-made toffee and apple fritters. Just as easily lost or cast aside are those titbits of culinary knowledge that make the difference between what is appetising and what is not: how to set about boiling beetroot; that the tops of young beet are a delicacy; that rhubarb should not be peeled; how to retain the delicate flavour of fish.

It is hoped that the accompanying anecdotes and old photographs will add zest and relish to the fare, vivid reminders of life in times past – so vivid that, not so much from a distance as just round a recently-turned corner, one hears the chant:

"Gravy and potatoes in a good brown pot,
Bake it in the oven and serve it very hot."

The last line of the couplet should probably be construed as an instruction; it is certainly more than a hint or an observation. My husband occasionally says I am dropping him a hint, while I maintain that I am merely making an observation. The following *observations* are based solely on my personal experience in the home; for me the best results often come from the easiest and simplest of approaches. Like a bunch of country flowers which arranges itself, sound meals don't need elaborate recipes. Silverside of beef, for instance, gently hammered and salted, placed on a bed of parsnips, slowly braised with one bay leaf and a cup of water, can be relied upon to produce a fine-flavoured, subtle dish every time.

Heavy cast iron and thick earthenware dishes slow-cook to perfection and bring out full flavour, and deserve a good oven cloth. Wiping up spills as they happen is a good idea; so is cleaning up as you go along and jotting the name of an emptied bag or packet on a memory board fixed to the kitchen wall. When my children were pre-school age we had a blackboard fixed to the whole of one wall in the kitchen. It provided fair interchange of ideas in a warm spot where I could keep an eye on them. I remembered how much I had learned that way from my mother – everything from nature to trimming pastry; wonderful years in which to soak up impressions and detail and have a confident start at school.

If you are worried about nutrition for faddy appetites, add wheat germ to crumbly toppings for casseroles and baked dishes, in meat loaf, stuffing, cereals or in sandwich spreads. Use honey liberally as a sweetener instead of white sugar, in desserts or sauces; trickle it onto muesli, banana, grapefruit, and give plenty of fresh fruit and organically grown vegetables. To buy fresh and eat fresh ensures peak vitamin value and flavour. Tune in to Radio Hints on Market Intelligence. Potatoes for baking in their jackets should have unblemished skins, without a suspicion of green, and be equal in size. Scrub gently in lukewarm water and rinse in cold; prick all over with the prongs of a fork. Bake for one hour or until soft. Serve split open with a pat of butter. Good to remember on the fifth of November as it's not always easy to cook potatoes gypsy style in the embers of the bonfire.

Brussels sprouts, carrots, cabbage or swedes pressure cooked and mashed with butter are delicious, all the flavour retained. Any liquid left from cooking, can be used as stock next day in soup.

Limp celery can be revived by standing it up to its leaves in salt water. Young beetroots should be well boiled with the tops and roots retained, otherwise they will bleed and lose their clear, distinctive colour. The skin slides off easily when sufficiently cooked. Larger beetroots are still good but take a lot of power to boil them well. Whole shelled hazel nuts, toasted in the oven, are very good on ice cream, stewed fruit etc. Their brown skins rub off easily between finger and thumb, if you desire them blanched.

A warmed knife blade does not drag meringue or cream nor spoil its appearance. Test a cake by pressing the top. A long, clean, thin skewer should emerge with no sticky, uncooked mixture on it. Sugary mixture cakes should be turned out of tins a few moments after taking them from the oven, otherwise they are difficult to remove. Soak the tins in cold water. To separate eggs, place an egg cup over the yolk, tilt the saucer and drain off the white. Alternatively, break the egg into a funnel; the white slips through. Make use of egg whites in sweets and savouries. Whisk into a jelly just about to set; use as meringue topping for plain milk pudding.

To ensure thorough cooking of pastry baked in glass ovenware, stand the dish on a metal sheet in the oven, which will conduct the heat through. This is especially important for custard pies and quiches.

Use greaseproof paper rather than polythene to rest on food. Foil is useful to cover sweets as it stands proud of the dish and does not disturb piped cream or cherries.

In jam making, to prevent any fermentation sprinkle a teaspoonful of caster sugar on top of the jam, immediately under the waxed disc, or dip the disc in brandy.

Use a long-handled wooden spoon to stir with and keep it steadily at the bottom of the preserving pan. Don't lift it about; this prevents scorching and breaking up of fruits. Grandmother used a round, wooden hazel stick which she called a thevil.

Gather fruit for jam and jelly making on a dry day. Raspberry jam is improved by adding ¼ pint of redcurrant juice to each pound of raspberries. Melting the sugar in the juice before adding the raspberries helps to keep the fruit whole.

One elderflower head, not too fully open, swished around in gooseberry jam, imparts a subtle flavour.

Use a thick pan for sauce making to prevent "catching". Milk used in savoury sauces can be pleasantly flavoured by infusing it with onion or bay leaf. Cooked rice can be flavoured by using tomato juice instead of water.

To prevent discolouration of apples and avocado pears, once cut, sprinkle well with lemon juice. Use a cut and break action for each piece of baking apple going into sauce or pie as this makes the fruit more "greshy", or juicy. Peeled apples should be dropped into water until used.

For a varied salad don't forget chopped nuts, sultanas, apple, diced beetroot, cream or cottage cheese, chives, chicory, parsley, coleslaw, decorated with radish "roses", tomato "lilies" and curled celery, spring onions poked in and cucumber thinly sliced all over.

Garnish roast duck with half slices of a very juicy orange and have an orange and watercress side salad.

Decorate drinks in hot weather with floating mint leaves, slivers of lemon, lemon slices slotted over the glass side, or small bunches of grapes. One of the most cooling of sweets is fresh-fruit salad. It looks mouth-watering dished up in scooped-out melon halves.

Stewed raisins and stewed prunes, slow-simmered in brown sugar and water, are more acceptable to children than medicine. Dip glace cherries in flour to prevent their sinking to the bottom of a fruit cake. Chives should be snipped rather than chopped and used fresh, not cooked, as an aid to digestion.

Use plenty of lemons and parsley; the latter has a high vitamin content and should be eaten, not merely regarded as decoration.

When boiling eggs, cover them with water, occasionally stir them gently and time them according to state required. (Average time is three minutes.) A spent match in the water helps to prevent shells cracking. Shell hardboiled eggs under running water. New-laid eggs are very difficult to shell. For this purpose they need to be kept a day or so beforehand.

Wrappings from butter and margarine can be kept in a stoppered jar and used for greasing cake tins.

The residue of white left in egg shells can be used for browning or glazing. Invert the half-shells on a handy saucer so that they drain.

The following temperatures are referred to in the recipes and should form a guide for modern ovens.

COOL OVEN	225–250°F	107–121°C
SLOW OVEN	275–300°F	135–149°C
MODERATE OVEN	375°F	190°C
HOT OVEN	425–450°F	218–233°C
VERY HOT OVEN	475–500°F	246–260°C

It is interesting to note the fire ovens or fire ranges of 1910 and thereabouts with no thermostats were well understood by the good Northern cook. Aunt Kate, an authority on the subject, before putting in a cake would thrust her hand well inside the oven and if she could allow it to remain there until she counted up to thirty it was the requisite degree of heat. If she had to withdraw her hand before then it was too hot. In order to lower the flames salt was sprinkled on the fire. The oven door was not opened for at least twenty minutes after the cake was put in, and when it was opened it was *never* slammed shut.

Catherine Rothwell, 1979

Cakes and Scones

1. LANCASTER SPICE LOAF

¾ lb Self-Raising Flour
1 teaspoon of Nutmeg
1 teaspoon Cinnamon
1 teaspoon of Ginger
Pinch of Salt
½ lb. Butter
½ lb. Brown Sugar
½ lb Currants
½ lb Sultanas
2 ozs. Chopped Mixed Peel
2 ozs. Chopped Almonds
4 ozs. Glace Cherries
3 Eggs
Milk

Sift flour; add spices and salt; rub in the butter till the mixture is crumbly. Stir in sugar, currants, sultanas, cherries, almonds and peel. Add the beaten eggs and enough milk to give a dropping consistency. Bake for two hours in loaf tins at 350°F.

'Pepper' and 'Bias'. Two buskers who entertained in front of Lancaster Town Hall in the early 1900s.

2. CHORLEY CAKES

1 lb. Rich Shortcrust Pastry
4 ozs. Washed and Dried Currants
Icing Sugar

Roll the pastry out ¼ inch thick and cut into four rounds about the size of a dinner plate. Place the currants centrally in these circles; moisten the edges and fold together. Press and roll out until the currants show through the pastry. Bake for thirty minutes at 350°F and sprinkle with icing sugar.

This is very similar to Belthorn Sad Cake which had sugar added with the currants (plus a little water) and was baked in a fire oven. The sugar gently bubbled out and made a brown, shiny topping. A soft, crumbly texture was retained which I find quite impossible to produce in a modern electric or gas oven. Sad Cake just has to have a fire oven to give it perfection.

3. TOSSET CAKES

1 lb. Plain Flour
1 lb. Butter
¼ lb. Raw Cane Sugar
1 Teaspoon Caraway Seeds
1 Teaspoon Coriander Seeds

Crush the seeds with a rolling pin or pestle. Rub the butter into the flour. Add sugar and crushed seeds and leave in a cool place overnight then roll out to ¼ inch thickness. Using a pastry cutter, place the small cakes on a floured baking sheet, sprinkling each with caster sugar. Bake in a cool oven for one hour until firm. The cakes should *not* brown. Dredge thickly with icing sugar when cool and store in an air-tight tin.

These spicy, sugary cakes were eaten in Stalmine the weekend after August 12th, on Tosset Sunday. The old name of the church was St. Oswald and "Tosset" makes affectionate reference to the saint.

4. CLUB CAKES

12 ozs. Plain Flour
8 ozs. Butter
3 ozs. Sugar

The butter and sugar are creamed, the flour worked in either by hand or using a food mixer, and when the dough is rolled out the small cakes can be cut. Baking is in a moderate oven, the finished cakes being liberally sprinkled with icing sugar.

The Pack Horse Inn, Stalmine. See recipe 3, Tosset Cakes.

5. TRUNNAH CHOCOLATE CAKE

4 ozs. Butter
2 ozs. Cocoa
4 ozs. Flour
2 Eggs
4 ozs. Soft Brown Sugar
Milk
Pinch of Salt
Glace Cherries and Flaked Almonds

Cream the butter and sugar until fluffy. Gradually add the eggs, sifted flour, salt and cocoa with sufficient milk to make a dropping consistency. Place in a well-greased circular tin and bake in a moderate oven for 25 minutes. When cool, cover with melted milk chocolate and decorate immediately with flaked almonds and cherries. Real Morello cherries are a special treat, but don't give your husband too many. Henry VIII liked cherries.

The Trunnah shops used to put their advertisements in rhyme. J. Clarke of Bridge Terrace wrote:

"Cakes from Trunnah so delight us,
That they make our tea sublime,
And departing make our minds up,
That we go to Clarke's next time."

The nearby family butcher, James Keirby, on Trunnah Road, Thornton, was famous for his pickled tongues and likewise waxed lyrical about them.

6. AUNTIE ALICE'S VICTORIA SANDWICH

2 Eggs
4 ozs. Caster Sugar
4 ozs. Butter
4 ozs. Self-Raising Flour

Beat the butter and sugar until light and creamy. Beat in the eggs gradually with some of the flour to prevent a curdled appearance. Gradually stir in the rest of the flour with a metal spoon. Have ready two sandwich tins, warmed, well greased and lined. Divide the mixture equally between them. Place side by side on the first runner of the oven and bake at 350°F. Cool on a wire tray and sandwich the two cakes together with home-made raspberry jam or lemon cheese. Sprinkle liberally with icing sugar.

A delightful rural scene. Axe sharpening on an oldfashioned grindstone. This couple remind me so much of my own Aunt Alice and Uncle Teddy. See recipe 6, Aunt Alice's Victoria Sandwich.

7. PARKIN

2 Cups of Wholemeal Flour
¾ Cup of Demerara Sugar
4 ozs. Butter
2 Tablespoons Syrup
1–2 Teaspoons (rounded) Ginger
1 Teaspoon Bicarb. of Soda
Pinch of Salt
1 Egg beaten with a little milk

Place dry ingredients together. Melt butter and syrup over gentle heat; add to mixing bowl. Add sufficient egg and milk mixture to produce a dropping consistency. Bake in a greased tin lined with greaseproof paper in a moderate oven. If stored for a few days before cutting, the flavour improves.

Father's opinion was that a drop of water added to the egg and milk mixture improved the flavour and another of his refinements was to substitute half a cup of fine oatmeal for half a cup of the wholemeal flour. The "ambrosial" touch was produced by finely chopped, crystallised or stem ginger tossed onto the mixture just before it was popped into the oven.

8. BURY SIMNEL CAKE

1 lb. Flour
2 ozs. Candied Peel
½ lb. Raw Cane Sugar
1 lb. Currants
½ lb. Sultanas
1 Teaspoon of Mixed Spice
½ Cup of Warm Beer
4 ozs. Chopped Almonds
3 ozs. Butter
2 ozs. Lard
4 Eggs
½ Teaspoon Bicarb. of Soda
1 lb. Almond Paste

Rub fat into flour. Add all the dry ingredients then beat in the eggs and beer, but reserve some of the egg for glazing the almond paste later. Bake in the centre of a moderate oven for about three hours. Cool. Roll out two-thirds of the almond paste to fit the cake, crimping the edges with a fork and fixing it on with runny jam. Make a dozen "eggs" from the remainder of the paste and balance them round the edges, brushing all the paste with the egg reserved. Brown under the grill and decorate with a fluffy, model Easter chicken.

Traditionally this was prepared four weeks beforehand to be eaten on Simnel or Mothering Sunday, mid-Lent. There was always an annual fierce argument in the kitchen that this version was not real Bury Simnel because the paste was not in the middle of the cake. Mother put the paste on top because if placed in the centre the cake became sad.

9. DROP SCONES

4 Cups Self-Raising Flour
2 Tablespoons of Light Golden Syrup
Pinch of Salt
½ Pint of Buttermilk or Milk
3 Heaped Tablespoons of Sugar
2 Eggs

Put flour, syrup, sugar and salt into a warmed bowl; add milk and beaten eggs. Whisk together until mixture is like thick cream. Heat up a greased "griddle" or girdle or heavy frying pan. Drop tablespoons of the mixture at evenly-spaced intervals on the hot griddle. Until you get used to dropping the amount of mixture it is as well to try them singly. When bubbles appear and the bottom is golden brown, turn over and cook the other side of the scone. Serve with butter or whipped cream.

Drop Scones with strawberry jam were served at the Manor, Poulton-le-Fylde, a country mansion which was a favourite wagonette drive for trippers in the early twentieth century from Blackpool and Lytham. Time was allowed to look round the ancient church of St. Chad with its picturesque grounds, replete with trees and leaning gravestones, even then centuries old. People still drive out to see the glorious carpet of snowdrops and crocuses each Spring.

10. AUNT KATE'S CAKE

4 Teacupfuls of Flour
2 Teacupfuls Sugar
6 ozs. Butter
1 Teaspoon Baking Powder
6 Eggs
A little fresh milk

Mix all the dry ingredients together. Beat the sugar and butter to a cream. Beat the yolks of the eggs and add to the beaten butter and sugar. Now add gradually to this semi-liquid mixture all the dry ingredients, beating all the time.

Next, beat the whites of the eggs to a stiff froth and incorporate with the cake, mixing all well together for ten minutes. Add sufficient milk to make a thick consistency. The excellence of the cake depends on the thoroughness of the mixing and beating. Bake in a moderate oven. Aunt Kate's Cake was decorated with rough almonds cast on before putting in the oven.

11. LANCASHIRE THRODKIN

1 lb. Coarse Oatmeal
6 ozs. Lard
Good pinch of salt

Rub lard into oatmeal and salt. Mix with a little water. Put into a shallow dish and cook in a slow oven with pieces of bacon cut into strips and placed on top. Eat hot. If any left, it can be broken up, spread with golden syrup and eaten cold instead of cereal for breakfast.

Men and their machines; a fine example of a threshing engine, taken in the 1920s when Lancashire Throdkin was still common on the Fylde.

Drinks

12. MEAD or HONEY BEER

5 lbs. Honey
¼ oz. each of Bay Leaves, Thyme, Rosemary
1 oz. each of Mace, Nutmeg and Sliced Ginger
½ Teacupful of Malt
2 ozs. Yeast
3 Gallons of Water

Boil the honey in two gallons of water for ¾ of an hour. Take the bay leaves, thyme, rosemary and boil for ¾ of an hour in the other gallon of water. Put this into a tub or earthenware crock with the malt. Stir frequently and when it is lukewarm, strain it. Pour it back into the tub and add the honey and water. Spread the yeast on pieces of toast and lay it on the surface. When the surface is covered with yeast, skim it off. Put the mixture in a barrel. Bruise the mace, nutmeg and sliced ginger; tie them in a piece of muslin and suspend them in the mixture by a piece of string. The mead will take about 48 hours to settle. It is then ready for use.

13. GRANDAD'S HERB BEER

In two gallons of water boil a few handfuls of the fresh young plants of stinging nettle, a few handfuls of dandelions and 2 ozs. of bruised ginger. (Nowadays it goes without saying that you must be particular about where you gather your nettles and dandelions and they must be thoroughly cleansed.) Boil all together for half an hour and strain. Place into it some pieces of toasted bread on which has been spread a small quantity of brewer's fresh yeast. When the process of fermentation is over add 1 oz. cream of tartar. (Grandad kept his "brew" by the fire oven to help the process.) Strain, bottle and cork the beer. He always used screw-top stone jars for this; never glass bottles. The were then laid on their sides in a cool place and the herb beer was ready for use within a few days. When I was about four I saw him open a jar. The screw top took off like a genie and herb beer spattered the ceiling. I was very impressed.

14. ELDERBERRY WINE

8 lbs. Ripe, Black Elderberries
1 gallon Water
3 lbs. Demerara Sugar
½ teaspoon Whole Allspice
1 oz. Ground Ginger
1 teaspoon Cloves
1 oz. Yeast
Slice of Toast

Strip the elderberries from their stalks. Pour the water over them. Mash the fruit well and leave for five days to extract all the juice, stirring well every day. Strain juice into preserving pan with sugar, allspice, ginger and cloves and boil for half an hour. Allow to cool and strain. Spread the yeast on a piece of toast; float it on top of the liquid; cover and leave to ferment for a week, stirring daily. Skim; strain off into a cask and leave the bung loose until fermentation has ceased. Then hammer the bung in tightly; leave for four months and then bottle.

15. RASPBERRY VINEGAR

Cover a large dish of raspberries with sugar and allow to stand for 24 hours or more till you can drain one pint of juice. Set aside. Stir into the strained fruit one pint of vinegar; strain again and add the liquid to the juice you set aside. Add two pounds of sugar. Simmer gently until syrupy. Allow to cool. Bottle when cold. The syrup may be used on pancakes instead of lemon, taken in hot water as a remedy for a cold, or put on plain vanilla ice cream.

16. ORANGEADE

4 Oranges
6 ozs. Sugar
1½ pints Water

Wash and dry the oranges. Thinly remove the zest from one orange. Put zest and sugar in a jug. Boil with ½ pint of the water. Stir until the sugar has dissolved. Cover and allow to infuse. Add the remaining cold water and the juice squeezed from the oranges. Don't leave the juice standing for long as it loses in vitamin C content. Strain into a glass jug.

17. COFFEE LIQUEUR

Grind 3 ozs. of best, freshly roasted coffee. Prepare a syrup with 1 lb. of sugar and half a pint of water. Put the coffee into the boiling syrup and boil for a few seconds. Mix all with one quart of brandy. Cork well and let it stand for one month. Filter and the liqueur is ready for use.

18. DAMSON GIN

This old recipe requires:

3 lbs. Damsons
3 lbs. Sugar
1 Large Bottle of Gin

Place well washed damsons in a large jar with a screw top. Put sugar over the top and pour the gin over. Screw down and keep until Christmas, then pour off the liquid and bottle.

19. APRICOT DRINK

A new recipe, using 4 oz. dried apricots, 1 pint of milk, 2 tablespoons of Grand Marnier.

Cover washed apricots with milk and leave to soak overnight in a cold place. Pour into goblet of electric mixer. Blend and strain. Add the Grand Marnier, slowly stirring in well.

Doorway at Beaumont Fishery, Skerton. The distinctive lintel is now in the Lancaster Museum collection.

Fish

20. LUNE SALMON

2 good-sized Tail Ends of Salmon
2 tablespoons of Snipped Chives

Put the fish into a pan and cover with water. Bring to the boil and simmer for five minutes only. Take out of the pan; save the liquor. Remove the skin and bones from the fish. Cut it into fair-sized pieces. Put it back into the pan with two cups of the fish stock and the chives. Cover and simmer very slowly for twenty minutes. Serve with cucumber and sprigs of parsley. Don't forget to eat the parsley. It is said to be good for kidney complaints.

21. EEL PIE

3 lbs. Eel skinned and cut up
4 tablespoons of Corn Oil or Olive Oil
6 ozs. of Chopped Onion
About 20 Button Mushrooms
Salt and Pepper
Butter and Flour
Lemon to garnish

Toss the eel in flour seasoned with salt and pepper. Brown the eel pieces in a pan containing hot oil. Take out the eel and lightly saute the onion. Return the eel slices to the pan; add the mushrooms, seasoning and a pint of water. Simmer for thirty minutes. The eel sauce can be thickened by gradually adding small lumps of butter, kneaded with flour, stirring all the time to keep it smooth. Serve hot, garnished with slices of lemon.

Eel pie is cooked as above, put in a pie dish, covered with a pastry top and baked at 400°F for thirty minutes.

A member of a Fleetwood family that dates back to when the town began in 1836 has described eel-spearing in the many ponds which used to line the areas of Broadway, Hambleton, Over-Wyre. The eels, caught with a long-poled, metal tri-pronged implement, were stuffed in a bag and towards evening taken home for stewing or making into pie.

22. HERRINGS

Herrings, once so plentiful and cheap they were a nourishing standby for poor people, have now become both scarce and expensive. The tasty, humble kipper, derived from the herring, is approaching the smoked salmon class.

Good Manx kippers soaked overnight in lemon juice need no further cooking. After draining off the liquid, remove the bones; mash the kippers with a little butter. Spread on brown bread; it tastes good. Cooking on a gridiron over a glowing, open fire or charcoal brings out the best in any kipper. Serve with scrambled egg.

Fresh herrings can be baked or grilled after rolling in oatmeal, like trout. A typical workman's meal sixty years ago was prepared as follows:

Clean and fillet six herrings. Roll them up and pack tightly into an earthenware, fireproof dish on top of three bay leaves. Sprinkle thickly with finely chopped onions. Cover with a white vinegar and water solution (half a cup of each). Cover with a lid and bake in a moderate oven for 40 minutes. If left overnight in the liquid, these can make a delicious and nourishing breakfast.

Boot-blacks and others outside Fleetwood Ferry landing in the 1900s. From here fishing trips could be undertaken. See recipe 21, Eel Pie.

A full load: The Victoria Horse Bus has stopped near Sulby Glen, Isle of Man. Possibly the party had herrings for breakfast. See recipe 22.

23. KILLINGTON FRIED TROUT

Clean, scale and remove fins, tail etc. with sharp, kitchen scissors. Do not split open. Dip in oatmeal, salt and pepper. Heat some butter in a heavy frying pan; lay in the trout and brown well. Serve thickly strewn with minced, fresh parsley and lemon quarters.

24. SCALLOPED LOBSTER

If you are fortunate enough to obtain a fresh lobster, treat it as directed in 1883.

1 Fresh Lobster
Bread Crumbs
Pepper, Salt, Butter
2 Pints of Stock

"Crack up the lobster and simmer in the stock for about half an hour. Add some Lancashire Relish, chopped shallott and chopped parsley. Cool. Extract the lobster meat; arrange in scallop shells; sprinkle with bread crumbs and dot with butter. Place in oven till lightly browned". Nowadays, placed under the grill and served immediately would perhaps be more convenient.

25. LANCASHIRE LOBSTER

A new way with lobster, for a special occasion, is to make it into a souffle.

1 Lobster
1 Pint water
1 Onion
1½ ozs. Flour
1½ ozs. Butter
1 Tablespoon Chives
½ oz. Gelatine
¼ Pint Double Cream
3 Egg Whites

Remove flesh from the lobster and place in a bowl. Crush shell and simmer in water for one hour with the onion. Strain off and keep. Melt butter; stir in flour; add stock; put in the snipped chives and flaked lobster. Dissolve the gelatine in a little hot water and add to the gently simmering lobster mixture, but do not boil. Cool well. Stir in the cream and fold in the stiffly beaten egg whites, making sure that no grease of any kind is on the bowl or the beater and that not a speck of yolk has wandered in. Chill and serve in a souffle dish.

26. POTTED SHRIMPS

Morecambe Bay shrimps have been prized as delicacies for three hundred years.

1 lb. Fresh Shrimps
5 ozs. Clarified Butter
¼ teaspoon Cayenne Pepper
Sea Salt

Put the shrimps in boiling water and cook for two minutes. Cool and remove from shells. Melt 3 ozs. of the clarified butter with cayenne and salt. Put the shrimps in an oven-proof dish and pour the seasoned butter over them. Bake for thirty minutes (350°F.). Remove from oven; drain and cool. Pack the shrimps into small jars; pour over the strained butter in which they were cooked. Leave to set, then cover with the remaining clarified butter – about ¼ in. thick.

27. FLEETWOOD BATTERED SHRIMPS

An old Fleetwood recipe tosses freshly-picked shrimps into batter and fries them immediately; they are eaten straight from the pan.

28. APPLE FRITTERS

The New Royal Cook Book of 1921 has a recipe for these, the batter for which may be used for coating shrimps.

Take a cup of flour, half a teaspoon of baking powder, one egg, a quarter teaspoon of salt and two-thirds of a cup of milk. Sift the dry ingredients; add beaten egg with milk; beat until smooth.

Invalid Foods

29. EGG FLIP

Break a fresh, free-range egg into a cup. Add one or two tablespoonfuls of milk and a little brown sugar. Beat until frothy. Strain into a tumbler and serve.

Milk and milk drinks are good if the invalid will tolerate them. So are freshly squeezed fruit juices, especially lemonade made from fresh fruit. Rosehip syrup, barley water and consomme soups are also suitable, but do not press anything if the invalid does not fancy it. Ray knobs cooked in milk with seasoning make a light, nourishing lunch. Eggs, white meat and light sponge puddings or finger biscuits are fairly easy to digest, but avoid all fried foods, very new bread, fatty foods, heavy cheese and NEVER re-heat foods. The latter is a good rule all the time. Lots of fluids, love and patience work wonders.

30. STEAMED EGG

1 Egg
½ oz. Butter
1 tablespoon of Milk
¼ teaspoon of Salt
1 pinch of Pepper

Grease a cup well with the butter; add the milk; break the egg and drop it in, sprinkling over with seasoning. Place the cup in a saucepan and pour round, enough boiling water to come up half way. Boil slowly for ten minutes; turn the egg out onto a hot plate and serve at once.

31. OATMEAL PORRIDGE

¼ cup of Medium Oatmeal
1 cup of Water
Pinch of Sea Salt

Boil the water in a saucepan and as it comes to the boil, stream in the oatmeal, stirring all the time. Cover and simmer gently for ten minutes, then add the salt and stir well. Simmer for another ten minutes. Serve hot in individual bowls of cold milk with a sprinkling on top of Demerara sugar or raw cane sugar.

32. TREACLE POSSET

A teaspoonful of treacle stirred into a teacupful of warm milk is good for a cold. A teaspoonful of honey stirred into warm milk is very good for getting an excitable child off to sleep.

33. BARLEY WATER

Boil half a teacup of pearl barley in one breakfast cup of cold water. Let it simmer gently for half an hour. Pare the yellow rind thinly off a fresh lemon and put it into a jug. Strain the barley water into the jug and let it infuse for ten minutes with a lid or piece of paper over the jug. It is then ready for drinking.

34. LEMON AND HONEY

Pour hot water over a tablespoonful of honey in a beaker. Add the juice of two or three lemons. Drink at regular intervals to soothe and heal a sore throat. For the same purpose use Raspberry Vinegar.

35. BEEF TEA

One pound of lean Shin Beef and one pint of cold water. Chop the beef finely and add to the water. Bring slowly to boiling point. Place all in a stone jar, tying a clean cloth tightly over the top. Place this jar in a pan of water which covers it within an inch of the top. Simmer slowly for three hours, replenishing water as necessary. Half a teacupful of pearl barley can also be added if desired.

This old recipe, a great standby in our house in the 20's and 30's, is now declared by some authorities to have little nutritional value. The way my mother made it (cooked slowly on the hob) brought out a delicious flavour and we four children clamoured for it, ill or well. Beef stew with a cowheel was another so-called "strengthener".

36. CHICKEN BRAWN

3½ lbs. Boiling Fowl
2 Pigs' Trotters
2 hard-boiled Eggs
Mixed Herbs
Sea Salt and Pepper

Place the fowl in a pan with the trotters, salt, pepper and mixed herbs. Cover with water and bring to the boil. Remove to the oven. In a large, lidded, oven-ware dish, it can then be cooked at 300°F for four hours. When cool, strip off all meat from chicken and trotters, chop finely, taste a morsel to be sure seasoning balance is correct. Return the meat to the liquid and heat through. Line a wet, deep dish with the sliced, hard-boiled eggs and gently pour in the meat, pressing down well. Leave to cool; cover with a sheet of greaseproof paper, then press under a weight for several hours. When set, it can be turned out, garnished with watercress and sliced up for a family meal.

37. CHICKEN BROTH

Joint the fowl. Put in a saucepan and cover with cold water. Boil gently for ¾ hour then add a dessertspoonful of rice, finely chopped parsley and seasoning (sea salt, celery salt, pepper). Boil for another half hour; skim and serve with squares of toast.

Flooded streets in a northern town in 1927. Chicken broth would not come amiss after this experience.

All the fun of the fair. Children enjoying themselves at Churchtown in the 1900s, each no doubt with a stick of toffee to chew. See recipe 50, Cottage Candy.

38. BRAMBLE JELLY

We made this in the days before crop spraying, gathering the wild blackberries in the heart of the country. Nowadays you must be certain that hedges in which the brambles grow (often field boundaries) have not been sprayed, and do not take berries from roadsides where petrol fumes may have coated the fruit with lead.

Gather the berries on a dry day, allowing half a pound of sugar to one pound of fruit and boil for ¾ of an hour. One pound of apples added to three pounds of berries improves the flavour, but where apples are used more sugar must be given (¾ lbs. of sugar to every pound of fruit).

Strained through a jelly bag (before sugar is added) produces a smaller yield for potting, but the resultant clear jelly looks beautiful and tastes fruity. This is also very good for colds in winter time as is blackcurrant jelly dissolved in a little hot water to make a drink.

Pickles, Sauces and Spreads

39. CHUTNEY

1 lb. Cooking Apples
1 teaspoon Sea Salt
1 lb. Green Tomatoes
1 lb. Onions
1 lb. Brown Sugar
2 pints White Vinegar

Peel and core the apples then chop them small with the onions and tomatoes. Pour on the vinegar, sugar and salt and stir it all up together. Cook until tender, stirring it at frequent intervals. Pot in clean jars or stoneware crocks and label.

Grandfather's pickled walnuts and red cabbage had a long preparation, committed to memory only. I recall the rows of green walnuts laid out in the sunshine, drying on the shed roof, and that he enjoyed this pickle with "collops" of best beef fried with onions.

40. PICKLED BEETROOT

Wash the beets, taking care not to prick or break any of the outside skin or fibres. Simmer in boiling water for –2 hours depending on size. Take out; allow to cool and slide skin off gently with the fingers. Slice and place in wide-mouthed jars. Boil vinegar and seasoning in the proportion of 2 ozs. whole pepper, 2 ozs. allspice to every gallon for ten minutes. Pour this liquid, when cold, onto the beets. Cover well.

41. PICKLED SAMPHIRE

Northern coast dwellers rave about pickled samphire. Although I have never tasted it myself, it sounds good, but not so if culled from a polluted coastline. If you find some growing fresh and clean (although much less plentiful, it still can be obtained on the salt marshes), this is what you do.

Wash it very well to remove all trace of grit or sand. Spread it out on a cloth in the sun and fresh air to dry. Put it in a pan with enough malt vinegar to cover the samphire and about one teaspoon of ground ginger. Allow it to boil until it changes colour and will slip off the stalk easily. Put it into jars and cover with vinegar. A prerequisite seems to be a true "sand grown" character to recognise the genuine article. In the old days samphire was gathered for sale in the towns and villages by country folk who had little other source of income. A Southport "sandgrounder" supplied the recipe.

42. BREAD SAUCE

Boil one medium onion stuck with cloves in a saucepan of 1½ cups of milk. Leave to stand for an hour. Strain off the liquid and mix it with six heaped tablespoons of white breadcrumbs. Return to heat; stir until thick and almost boiling. Add a teaspoon of butter and a tablespoon of cream when the mixture has cooled a little. Serve immediately with roast turkey or chicken.

43. COLE SLAW

Shred the heart of a firm Savoy cabbage very finely and cover with the following dressing:

Whisk two eggs in a jug with two tablespoons of milk and two tablespoons of brown sugar, ½ teaspoon of Pommery or plain mustard and a little sea salt, 8 ozs. of white vinegar and water. Stir constantly. Pour into the jug two tablespoons of melted butter; keep stirring over heat until the dressing thickens. Do not pour over the shredded cabbage until quite cold.

The Ship Inn, Freckleton. Ships and rum go together, and the inn was suspected of harbouring contraband in times past. See recipe 47, Rum Butter.

44. PEACH MARMALADE

2 lb. Prepared Peaches
1½ lbs. Sugar
2 tablespoons of Lemon Juice
1 teaspoon Brandy

Pare and stone peaches. Cut up small. Use really ripe fruit. The weight must be calculated after the fruit is prepared. Crack about one quarter of the stones; chop the kernels and cover with cold water. Leave. Place the cutup fruit in a preserving pan and heat slowly, stirring to prevent sticking, as no water is added. The juice will eventually run. Simmer for 45 minutes and add the sugar. Bring to the boil and boil for five minutes. Add two tablespoons of lemon juice and the water from the cracked stones and kernels. Boil for a further ten minutes or until a set is obtained. Pot and cool, covering with a waxed circle dipped in brandy.

45. NUT HONEY

Juice of 3 Oranges
Grated Rind of 1 Orange
1 oz. Butter
1 oz. Ground Almonds
6 ozs. Sugar
1 Egg Yolk

Cook all together in a double saucepan until the mixture looks like honey. Pot and cover. As a tea-time spread for children this is a winner.

46. SPICED NUTS

Shell, heat in butter, then toss in a salt spice mixture (cinnamon or ginger). Roasted hazelnuts lend themselves to this.

47. RUM BUTTER

½ lb. Moist Brown Sugar
¼ lb. Unsalted Butter
2 tablespoons of Rum
½ teaspoon of Nutmeg
¼ teaspoon of Cinnamon

Beat the butter over heat until soft and creamy but do not let it become oily. Mix the spices with the sugar and beat into the butter. Add the rum, beating in each addition. Put into a basin and cover when set. Serve from this basin. In the Lake District, special basins, beautifully decorated and kept in the family for years, were used only for this purpose although brandy, more often than rum, was put in the recipe.

Ready for a spin. The sandwiches are packed, the car awaits.

Seven little milkmaids, each with her pail. Girls at Staining School, 1905. Mary Gibson, standing next to the teacher on the right, became a dairy maid on her father's farm. *See recipe 56, Syllabub.*

48. DAD'S TREACLE TOFFEE

1 lb. Demerara Sugar
½ lb. Treacle
¾ lb. Butter
Small tub of Cream
2 tablespoons of Water
Pinch of Cream of Tartar

Put the water into a pan; add sugar and treacle and a small amount of the butter. Heat very slowly so as not to burn the mixture. Thinly slice the rest of the butter and add gradually with the cream of tartar. Bring to the boil. Test a small quantity by dropping into cold water. If it forms into a hard lump it is ready. Allow to cool down but not set. Stir in the cream and pour into a flat toffee tin or the kind in which you make Swiss Roll. It very quickly sets. You need a small toffee hammer to break it into mouth-sized pieces which can then be wrapped in screws of greaseproof paper.

This was always a great stand-by in foggy weather. Marching to school with a thick, one-foot-wide, woollen scarf tied cross-wise over your chest and secured at the back with a huge safety pin, you popped a piece of this toffee into your mouth to "keep out the cold" just as you stepped into the street. The day I tried to twirl the milk kit in a swift circle, attempting to defy the law of gravity but managing only to flood the passage floor (I had resisted the temptation for weeks) I didn't get any treacle toffee.

49. LEMON CHEESE

¼ lb. Butter
1 lb. Sugar
6 Eggs
Juice of Two Large Lemons

Grate the lemon rind. Have ready a pan of boiling water. Stand in this a stone jar or jug. Put in sieved sugar and butter. When melted, add well-beaten, strained eggs, grated rind and lemon juice. Stir continually until it thickens on back of wooden spoon. When fairly cool, pour into warmed, clean jars.

50. COTTAGE CANDY

1 lb. Soft Brown Sugar
¼ lb. Butter
4 tablespoons Milk

Melt ingredients over low light then boil gently until mixture thickens. Remove from heat and beat hard until creamy. Pour into buttered tray and mark into squares while still warm.

The photograph shows Mr and Mrs Rossall with one of their children, Baden, in front of Staining Windmill in 1904. The horses that pulled the ploughs in the fields close by feared the heavy, whirling sails and had to wear blinkers or, if they came right up to the mills, were blindfolded.

51. ORMSKIRK BRANDY SNAPS

2 ozs. Plain Flour
3 ozs. Caster Sugar
3 ozs. Golden Syrup
1 teaspoon Brandy
2 ozs. Butter
½ teaspoon Ground Ginger

Grease two baking sheets. Sift the flour and ginger. The butter, sugar and golden syrup should be gently melted in a saucepan. Take off the heat and stir in all the other ingredients. Place teaspoonfuls of this mixture on the baking sheets, allowing room for the mixture to spread. Bake at the top of the oven for ten minutes until golden-brown.* Allow to cool slightly; loosen and roll round the greased handle of a wooden spoon. The brandy snaps will then set in the traditional curled shape. A new way with brandy snaps would be to fill them with whipped cream. *At 350°F.

Sandwich fillings give much scope for the imagination. Different kinds of bread make for variety; some fillings taste specially good with brown bread; fresh watercress is good with coarse wholemeal. Use cheese and sausage, cottage cheese with chives, creamed soft-boiled egg, hard-boiled egg, boiled ham and pineapple, meat loaf, tomato with chutney, sliced capon with sage and onion stuffing, sliced tongue, cold roast lamb, lettuce and tomato. If you use cucumber, cut both bread and cucumber as thinly as possible and use as soon as possible. Slightly dampened paper layered over the sandwiches helps to keep them from drying up in hot weather. Scotch eggs make good filling extras. Thermos flasks are useful for carrying both hot and cold drinks.

52. MALT BREAD

1 lb. Self Raising Flour
1 cup Sultanas
1 Egg
1 cup brown Muscavado sugar
2 tablespoons Treacle
1 oz. Butter
1 tablespoon Malt

Mix the dry ingredients together. Add the treacle, beaten egg and malt with enough cold water to make a stiff batter. Bake in a loaf tin in a moderate oven. Next day, cut into slices and butter thickly.

53. NED FIELDEN'S BUN LOAVES

2 lbs. Plain Flour
4 ozs. Margarine
3 ozs. Currants
1 oz. Mixed Peel
2 ozs. Yeast
4 ozs. Sugar
1 teaspoon Salt
3 ozs. Sultanas
1 Egg
1 pint Milk and Water

Rub the margarine into the flour. Add the sugar, salt, currants, sultanas and peel. Make a well in the centre. Put in the yeast mixed with a little water and the whole egg. Stir in half of the warm milk and water and allow to stand for ten minutes. Knead to a light dough, using the remainder of the milk and water, and allow to stand again for ten minutes. Put into two, warmed, greased tins and allow to rise for twenty minutes. Bake in a moderate oven for about half an hour. When baked, brush over with sugar and milk to glaze.

In grandmother's day, the dough was placed in a large earthenware bowl, cream glazed inside, and set upon the warm hearthstone to rise.

Puddings and Pies

54. CUSTARD PUDDING

3 tablespoonfuls of Flour
3 Eggs
3 breakfast cupfuls of Milk

Put the flour into a bowl and make into batter with a little cold milk. Separate the yolks from the whites of eggs. Put the whites on a flat plate and beat to a froth with a flat, open-wire beater. Beat the yolks also and add them to the batter. Put the remainder of the milk in a saucepan to warm a little; add the batter and sugar to taste. Stir well till it boils. Boil for four minutes then lift off heat to cool a while. Add the whites, stirring them in lightly to keep froth on top. A drop of vanilla flavouring at this point is optional. The heat of the pudding cooks the whites sufficiently and gives a lovely texture to a nourishing, light pudding.

55. MARTHWAITE BAKED CUSTARD

1 pint Milk
4 tablespoons of Sugar
4 Egg Yolks
Vanilla to flavour
Nutmeg

The yolks and sugar should be beaten together and the milk boiled. Whilst still boiling pour over the yolk mixture and keep stirring. Turn into a large, buttered dish after straining. Bake in a moderate oven for 25 minutes. Sprinkle with the grated nutmeg. The mixture can be baked in a pastry case to form custard pie.

So useful is the egg, ancient symbol of fertility, that cooking would be difficult without it. The Mount at Fleetwood, once a huge sandhill, is one ot the many places in the north where the traditional rolling of decorated, hard-boiled eggs takes place every Easter Monday.

56. SYLLABUB

Old English Syllabub was made with milk straight from the cow into wine or cider to make a frothy mixture, sweetened, and flavoured with spices. In Tudor times the cow was milked out in the street or by the hedge. A newer method is to soak the grated rind of one lemon in its own juice for two hours, then add 3 ozs. of caster sugar, two tablespoons of brandy, two tablespoons of sherry. Gently add this mixture to half a pint of whipped double cream until all is blended. Put into goblets and chill before serving.

57. APPLE PIE

6 ozs. Shortcrust Pastry
1½ lbs. Cooking Apples
2–3 ozs. Demerara Sugar

Peel and core apples; cut and break into chunks; put half the apples in a pie dish; sprinkle with sugar; add the rest of the apples with two tablespoons of water. Cover the pie with rolled-out pastry; decorate with pastry leaf shapes and glaze with milk. Put the pie on a baking sheet in the centre of the oven preheated to 400°F. for 35 minutes.

In winter, when there was little variety for fruit pies, mother used figs as a filling. They were soaked overnight, cooked with brown sugar and cut into strips.

58. KIM'S APPLE PIE

This is a new variation in which the apples are pre-cooked and the pastry rolled very thinly (lining a pie plate and having a crust on top). A scattering of cinnamon, together with a handful of raisins, is added to the apple mixture. Worth making for the spicy scent in the kitchen alone during cooking time, but it tastes particularly delicious, the secret being in the *thin* quality of the pastry, the delicate browning and the succulence of apples redolent with spice.

Who couldn't knock the skin off a rice pudding?
Tough guys (and girls) ready for a race.

59. RICE PUDDING

The most important rule about rice pudding is not to buy it in a tin. There's no need for this sound, body-building food, properly made, to be at all boring. As an accompaniment to stewed apples or laced with rose hip syrup it's very good fare indeed.

Wash two tablespoonsfuls of pudding rice. Add one tablespoonful of brown sugar. (This makes the milk look appetisingly creamy.) Pour on a pint of milk and scatter ground nutmeg on the surface. Bake in a very moderate oven for 1½ hours until nicely "creeded".

60. SNOW PANCAKES

Grandmother's pancakes were made with the help of 3 tablespoonfuls of snow. Besides that she used:

3 tablespoonfuls of Flour
1 Egg
½ pint of Milk fresh from the cow
Lard for frying

Mix the flour with the milk by degrees and the egg well beaten, and (just before frying) the snow. It should then all be beaten up together quickly and put into the frying pan.

61. SLOW PANCAKES

This new, slower to make, recipe blends together two eggs, ½ pint of milk, ½ pint of water, 2 tablespoonfuls of melted butter, 3 ozs. of flour and a pinch of salt. The batter is then left to stand for an hour. A small, clean frying pan should be brushed with melted butter and a dessertspoon of the batter dropped in. Tilt the pan to spread it evenly; brown lightly and quickly over high heat. A heated dish can be filled with the pancakes, caster sugar dusted between layers, more melted butter poured over and finished off with a glass of brandy.

The ancient market town of Poulton-le-Fylde still rings the Pancake Bell on Shrove Tuesday. Traditionally it was rung by an apprentice to call the other apprentices from work and "prepare to eat their pancakes", which were begged from house to house in the village. The boy who ate the most pancakes was a champion.

62. ARLOUISE'S GINGER SPONGE

2 breakfast cups Flour
1 breakfast cup Sugar
1 teacup Milk
1 tablespoon Treacle
1 teaspoon Bicarbonate of Soda
1 tablespoon Syrup
1 teaspoon Ginger
1 tablespoon Butter
1 Egg

Rub the butter into the flour; add sugar, ginger, treacle, syrup. Beat up the egg; add it with the milk and stir well. Put the bicarb of soda in a tablespoon of boiling water and add to mixture whilst still fizzing. Beat the mixture for five minutes. Bake in a moderate oven for ¾ hour and serve with white sauce.

63. LEMON DELIGHT

2 ozs. Butter
4 ozs. Caster Sugar
1 Lemon
1 Egg
2 level tablespoonfuls Plain Flour
¼ pint Milk

Cream the sugar and butter. Stir in the lemon juice and grated lemon rind. Add the egg yolk. Stir in the flour and the milk. Whip the egg white stiffly and fold into the mixture. Pour into a greased 1 pint pie dish and stand the dish in a tray of cold water. Bake in a very moderate oven for one hour.

A tranquill scene. See recipe 61, Slow Pancakes.

64. PINEAPPLE PUDDING

2 ozs. Butter
2 ozs. Plain Flour
½ pint Milk
2 ozs. Sugar
2 Eggs
1 small tin Pineapple or better still, fresh pineapple crushed
4 ozs. Caster Sugar for the meringue

Melt the butter; add the flour and cook until the mixture leaves the side of the pan. Add the milk gradually, stirring all the time to make a thick sauce. Cool slightly. Stir in the sugar, egg yolks and pineapple juice. Reheat the sauce until it thickens again, stirring all the time. Chop the pineapple and put it into a greased pie dish. Cover with the pineapple sauce.

To make the meringue, beat the egg whites until stiff; add half the caster sugar. Beat again until the meringue stands up in peaks. Fold in the rest of the caster sugar. Cover the pineapple with the meringue and sprinkle with caster sugar. Cook in a slow oven until the meringue is crisp.

65. FRUIT CRUMBLE

1 lb. Soft Fruit (e.g. apples, plums)
5 ozs. Plain Flour
5 ozs. Sugar
3 ozs. Butter
3 ozs. Sugar

Stew the fruit with the 5 ozs. of sugar and allow to cool; pour into a heatproof dish. Rub the butter into the flour and stir in the 3 ozs. of sugar. Spread the mixture over the fruit. Bake in a moderately hot oven.

66. BARBER GREEN PUDDING

½ pint Milk
2 ozs. Sugar
1 oz. Butter
2 Eggs
Breadcrumbs (Reduce about half of a small loaf)
3 tablespoons Strawberry Jam
Cinnamon

Boil the milk, butter and sugar and pour over the breadcrumbs, egg yolk and scattering of cinnamon. Place in a greased pie dish and bake in a slow oven until set. Spread with the warmed jam. Beat the egg whites until stiff; fold in 1 oz. of caster sugar and pour onto the top of the pudding. Place in the oven to brown the delicious meringue topping. This is a lovely, light, summer pudding, improved further with a few fresh strawberries tossed into each serving.

Working up an appetite. See recipe 69, Savoury Balls & Stew. Corporal Ashton (right) and five colleagues at Hornby in 1910.

67. ROSY APPLES IN SYRUP

Six large, rosy apples, washed but not peeled. Remove the core from the base of the apple, retaining the stalk. Dissolve 2 ozs. of sugar in ½ pint of water to make the syrup. Put the apples with 3 tablespoonfuls of plum or raspberry jam into a casserole, then pour over the syrup and juice of a lemon. Stew gently till tender but whole. Lift the apples onto a hot dish; strain the syrup over them and scatter with blanched, shredded almonds.

68. VALLEY APPLE PUDDING

3 Eggs and the weight of these 3 eggs in Flour, Sugar and Butter

Cream the butter and sugar. Beat in the eggs, gradually at the same time adding the flour. Place well-chopped apples at the base of a large pudding basin and cover with the mixture. Steam for 2½ hours. Serve with custard. It is useful to have extra "dollops" of apple ready for those who complain they haven't got enough fruit. I make an extra saucepanful. Bramleys are ideal, gently stewed with brown sugar sufficiently long for them to "fall". Don't overcook. They can be kept warm under the hob in a fire-proof dish. The Valley refers to Rossendale where my mother was born.

Using the same mixture with a fistful of sultanas and currants added, arranged in individual bun tins and cooked for about twenty minutes in a moderate oven, will produce delicious fruit buns for tea or supper.

Soups and Savouries

69. SAVOURY BALLS & STEW

In a basin place half a pound of flour, 4 ozs. of shredded suet, a little minced parsley and chopped onion, salt and pepper. Mix together with a little cold water, sufficient to make a stiff dough; divide into balls; roll each lightly in flour and drop into a stew. Cook for one hour. A tasty stew can be made as follows:

½ lb. Beef cut into small squares
1 large Spanish Onion
1 Carrot
1 Turnip or small Swede
Celery Stick
pinch of Salt
Mixed Herbs
1 dessertspoonful of Pearl Barley

Simmer the meat for 1½ hours with the barley and herbs before adding the chopped vegetables and seasoning.

70. SHEEP'S HEAD BROTH

Place a sheep's head and trotters into a large bowl or can of salt and water and soak all night. In the morning scrape well, rinse in running water, place in a large pan and boil with sufficient water to cover, adding ¾ cup of barley, ¾ cup of peas, 1 small turnip cut into squares, 2 diced carrots, 2 blanched leeks, pepper and salt to taste. Boil for 3 or 4 hours then strain off the broth into a tureen and serve immediately.

Hog's head, sheep's head or boar's head could be the basis of a dish going back to the Vikings. In the sixteenth century and before there were no vegetables apart from peas and beans; bread ("maslin") was a mixture of coarse grain, rye and oats; sweetening consisted of honey from bees. The paddock at the "toft" or homestead had a patch of oats, barley or wheat. Herbs were used to mask the taste of meat "going off" and there was no fresh meat in winter except from pigeons kept for that purpose in a special pigeon house and these were for the Lord of the Manor and his family.

Mother hated preparing sheep's head but it had to be done because father roared for it like a Viking. It tasted good and I'm sure it was nourishing but I have never been bold enough to cook one myself or to make black puddings. Aunt Kate was not afraid to tackle ox heads and ox feet.

Bannocks, cooked on a girdle or griddle to go with either, come from "bruni" which is pure Norse.

71. SAVOURY FLAN

Line a tin or deep pie dish with pastry. Mince 4 ozs. cooked ham and onion. Add a pinch of sage and gently arrange the mixture in the uncooked pastry case. Skin a tomato by dropping it first into very hot water; cut it into slices and place it over the filling together with slices of hard-boiled egg. Sprinkle with chopped parsley. Beat one egg with one cup of milk and season it to taste. Pour this carefully and slowly over the mixture in the flan and bake in a moderate oven until set and nicely browned.

72. QUICHES

Cheesecakes and pastas have become very popular since more people have travelled abroad but they are only variations on original themes. Bought quiche is tasty but often has a wet bottom – unforgiveable in grandmother's day. A simple quiche can be made thus:

6 ozs. Shortcrust Pastry
2 ozs. Onion
4 ozs. Grated Lancashire Cheese
4 ozs. Chopped Mushrooms
¼ pint of Milk
2 tablespoons of Cream
Salt and Pepper
Chopped Parsley or Snipped Chives

Roll out the pastry and line a flan ring. Chop the onion finely and fry over gentle heat in butter till transparent. Gently cook the chopped mushrooms and arrange with the onions in the flan case. Whisk the eggs with the milk and cream; add the chopped parsley and spoon the mixture into the flan. Bake in centre of oven at 400°F. for 30 minutes, then reduce heat and bake for a further 10 minutes.

73. STEAK AND KIDNEY PIE

Two pounds of best beef steak are recommended in Grandma's recipe but you can "make do" with braising or stewing steak. Beat it with a hammer; cut thinly into squares and place in a pie dish with seasoning. Add a breakfast cup of cold water. Core and dice the kidney. Put all in the pie dish and cook slowly for three hours, placing a shortcrust pastry top on the dish in the last hour of cooking. Grandma used to roll the pieces of steak in finely-minced suet before putting them into the dish and I presume this helped in making the rich, brown, natural gravy. She also put the pastry lid on much earlier, covering with buttery paper if it browned before the meat was cooked. This method worked in the fire oven, but in a modern electric or gas oven the pastry would blacken and burn.

74. LANCASHIRE HOT POT

Some cooks now use stewing beef cut up into cubes to make hot pot, it being simpler to handle, but real hot pot is made using middle-neck lamb chops. It was always served with pickled red cabbage at our house.

8 Middle-neck Lamb Chops
4 Lamb Kidneys, sliced
½ lb. Sliced Onions
Salt and Pepper
½ pint Stock
2 lb. Sliced Potatoes

Trim excess fat from chops. Put a layer of potatoes in a deep, oven-proof dish; lay some of the chops on top; cover with a layer of kidneys and onion. Make similar layers, seasoning each with salt and pepper. Finish with a layer of potatoes. Pour over the stock and brush the potatoes with melted butter. Cover with a lid and cook in the oven for two hours at 350°F. Remove the lid; increase the temperature and cook for another thirty minutes to brown the potatoes. My mother used to add trimmed slices of bacon on top to crisp, at this stage. An updated version of hot pot is to add successive layers of tomatoes plus a bouquet garni then the final touch of bacon slices.

75. BAKED RABBIT

2 Jointed Rabbits
2 Eggs beaten well
4 ozs. Breadcrumbs
½ oz. Mixed Herbs
Sea Salt and pepper (freshly ground)

Coat the washed and dried joints with seasoned flour. Dip in the beaten eggs and coat with breadcrumbs and herbs; dot with butter. Place in a greased casserole and bake in the oven, removing at regular intervals to baste. Cook for two hours at 350°F.

"Aw loike a rabbit pie," wrote Lancashire dialect poet, Samuel Laycock in 1886, and an old recipe at that time was: Cut a rabbit into joints; wash and steep in water and salt for ten minutes. Remove as many of the large bones as possible and boil them in water. Line a deep pie dish with slices of ham and on this foundation lay the pieces of rabbit sprinkled with salt and the liver and kidneys. Add two hard-boiled eggs cut into slices and a cup of cold water. Bake in a moderate oven for an hour then place a pie crust over and bake for a further ½ hour, increasing oven temperature. Just before bringing to table carefully pour in through opening in pie crust the liquid in which the rabbit bones were cooked.

76. ROAST FYLDE CHICKEN

If obtainable, a fresh-killed, free-range bird, ready-dressed. Wash well under a cold-water tap at full force. Stuff with sage and onion or chestnut stuffing.

The shooting party at Wharles in 1897 shows James Shorrock, farmer, smoking pipe and beside him, holding the black dog, one of Lord Derby's gamekeepers, Mr Davies, whose son sits at the front with a spade.

Squeeze lemon juice over the bird and cover well with buttered, greaseproof paper. Place in a hot oven; keep well basted. The length of time for cooking varies with the size of the bird, but a good roaster is not likely to need more than two hours. Allow the last fifteen minutes with the paper removed to ensure even, gold browning of the skin. Serve with apple sauce and scrubbed potatoes cooked in their jackets or peeled and browned alongside the bird. Small sprouts touched with early frost are the best vegetable accompaniment to Fylde chicken. If a Spring chicken, serve with real, garden, pod peas and new potatoes.

77. ROAST PILLING LAMB

Before roasting, wash the joint of lamb and rub gently with coarse salt; pour over the juice of half a lemon and scatter with dried Rosemary leaves. The time required for cooking varies with the size of the joint. Pilling lamb is best served with fresh-made mint sauce, the recipe for which comes from nearby Preesall.

4 ozs. Mint Leaves; 6 ozs. Sugar; ½ pint Malt Vinegar

Chop the mint finely. Boil the vinegar; pour it on the mint and sugar. When the sugar has dissolved by stirring it with a wooden spoon, pour into wide-mouthed, clean jars almost to the brim. Allow to cool, then seal.

Quite a handful. See recipe 77, Roast Pilling Lamb.

78. BLACKBURN CHEESE AND ONION PIE

Line a pie plate with pastry. Fill with small pieces of cheese and grated onion. (Chopping produces less tears – or use a blender.) Add seasoning and a very little milk, only enough to moisten the cheese and onion mixture. Cover with a pastry lid. Bake in a hot oven for about ½ hour and serve hot.

79. LIVER AND BACON

1 lb. Liver
½ lb. Bacon
1 oz. Flour
2 Onions
Salt and Pepper
1 teaspoon Chopped Parsley
2 ozs. Dripping or Butter
½ pint cold water

Slice the liver ½ inch thick; wash thoroughly; dry and leave in a cloth for ½ hour before cooking. Fry the sliced bacon; dip the liver in half of the flour and all the seasoning. Fry along with slices of onions and remove to a hot dish. Add the rest of the flour to the pan; pour in the water, stirring well with chutney to make an appetising colour and use this as gravy, serving the liver on top of the bacon.

80. STUFFED TOMATOES

Use large, ripe tomatoes
½ lb. finely-minced, lean Steak
Onion, Parsley
1 teaspoon mixed, dried herbs and seasoning
Knobs of Butter
Left-over mashed Potato

Cut a slice from the top of each tomato. Remove seeds and scoop out some of the pulp; drain. Mix the meat, grated onion, chopped parsley, herbs and seasoning with the tomato pulp and carefully stuff the tomatoes with the savoury mixture. Place a layer of mashed potato over the top of each; dot with butter and bake in a moderate oven for 25 minutes. Sprigs of parsley or cress can be used to garnish. Served with fresh garden peas or braised celery hearts, they are delicious as an evening snack.

81. POTATO SCONES

Take 2 cups of boiled, mashed potatoes, 1 cup of flour, 3 tablespoons of melted butter. Add the butter and as much flour as is needed; this varies according to the kind of potato, but don't make the mixture too dry. Brush with milk and brown under grill.

82. TRIPE AND ONIONS

When King Cotton reigned in Lancashire, every village and city had its tripe shop. Tripe and onions was reckoned a nourishing, cheap dish for the workers and tripe-dressers probably outnumbered fish and chip shop proprietors. My uncle, who became Treasurer in a London borough, made an annual pilgrimage back to his native Lancashire for the express purpose of dining off tripe and onions. Here's how mother made it after we children returned laden from the shop in Whittaker Lane, Heaton Park.

2 lbs. Dressed Tripe
¾ lb. Sliced Onions
1½ pints Milk
2 ozs. Butter
1 oz. Flour
Nutmeg, Seasoning

Cut the tripe into narrow strips about 2 inches long. Simmer the tripe and onions in the milk for about one hour until tender. Melt the butter in a pan; stir in the flour and cook for a few minutes. Gradually add the milk from the tripe to make a thick sauce. Bring to the boil and season with nutmeg and salt. Add the tripe and onions; heat through and serve with mashed potatoes.

83. POTATO PIE

We adored this meal and never grew tired of it. Baked in the fireoven, Potato pie with a thick, brown crust was accompanied with freshly boiled young beetroot in vinegar, pickled red cabbage or pickled walnuts (all homemade and prepared by father).

1 lb. Stewing Steak
4 ozs. Chopped Onions
¾ pint Stock
1 dessertspoon Chopped Parsley
Salt and Pepper
2 lbs. Sliced Potato
1 lb. Pastry for Crust

Chop the meat into cubes; add the onions, stock, parsley, salt, pepper and put all into a deep, earthenware, pie dish; cover and slow cook in the oven for two hours, after which time remove the lid; cover with the thinly-sliced potatoes and pastry. Bake until well risen and brown, increasing oven temperature to 375°F.

84. BEEF AND HAM ROLL

1 lb. Lean Shoulder Steak
½ lb. Ham
1 beaten Egg
1 cup Breadcrumbs
Seasoning
1 teaspoon Chopped Parsley

Mince the ham and steak and mix with the breadcrumbs, seasoning and chopped parsley. Bind with the beaten egg. Steam in a greased pudding basin for 3½ hours. This goes very well with buttered swedes or carrots well mashed and chopped, boiled onions or spinach.

85. GRANNY BROWN'S BRAISED OX TONGUE

Wash and dry one salted ox-tongue, after soaking in water overnight. Prepare a mirepoix of vegetables (2 carrots, 2 small turnips, 2 onions, stick of celery, salt, 2 cloves, bouquet garni, 1 oz. of dripping or butter).

Heat the dripping or butter and add the vegatables, washed and cut into small pieces. Fry gently. Add the bouquet garni and place all in an earthenware dish. Put the tongue on it and pour over 2 pints of brown stock which has been brought to the boil. Cover with greaseproof paper. Put the lid on the earthenware dish and place in a hot oven. After about ten minutes reduce the heat and cook very slowly for about five hours until the tongue is tender. Remove from dish; cut away gristle; pull out any bones or skin. If the tongue is adequately cooked, the skin peels away very easily. Put the tongue into a round tin or casserole; cover with one pint of the stock to which has been added ¼ oz. of gelatine. Put a piece of greaseproof paper over and a weight upon it. After allowing to stand thus for 24 hours, it can be turned out and served sliced with dressed salad.